THE REAL DEAL

TOBACCO

Rachel Lynette

Heinemann
LIBRARY

www.heinemann.co.uk/library
Visit our website to find out more information about Heinemann Library books.

To order:

 Phone 44 (0) 1865 888112

 Send a fax to 44 (0) 1865 314091

Visit the Heinemann bookshop at www.heinemann.co.uk/library to browse our catalogue and order online.

First published in Great Britain by Heinemann Library, Halley Court, Jordan Hill, Oxford OX2 8EJ, part of Pearson Education.

Heinemann is a registered trademark of Pearson Education Ltd.

© Pearson Education Ltd 2008
First published in paperback in 2009
The moral right of the proprietor has been asserted.

Editorial: Nancy Dickmann
Design: Richard Parker and Tinstar Design Ltd
Illustrations: Darren Lingard
Picture Research: Mica Brancic and Frances Topp
Production: Alison Parsons

Originated by Chroma Graphics
Printed and bound in China by Leo Paper Group

ISBN 978 0 431 90732 1 (hardback)
12 11 10 09 08

10 9 8 7 6 5 4 3 2 1

ISBN 978 0 431 90739 0 (paperback)
13 12 11 10 09

10 9 8 7 6 5 4 3 2 1

British Library Cataloguing in Publication Data
Lynette, Rachel.
  Tobacco. - (The real deal)
1. Tobacco use - Health aspects - Juvenile literature
2. Tobacco - Juvenile literature
I. Title
613.8'5

A full catalogue record for this book is available from the British Library.

Acknowledgments
The publishers would like to thank the following for permission to reproduce photographs:
Alamy/Aliki Image Library/Kathleen Watmough p. **4**; Bubbles p. **19**; Corbis pp. **12** (Zefa/Alan Schein), **14** (Ramin Talaie), **16** (Bettmann), **17** (James Leynse), **18** (Jerry Arcieri), **21** (Zefa/Michael A. Keller), **23** (Michael Reynolds); Getty Images pp. **5** (Photographer's Choice/Garry Gay), **9** (Stone+/Karen Moskowitz), **13** (AFP/Pedro Armestre); Mediscan p. **11**; Photolibrary. com/Index Stock Imagery/Mike Robinson p. **27**; Rex Features pp. **22** (Ventureli), **24** (Andy Paradise), **25** (Buzz Pictures/Roger Sharp); Science Photo Library pp. **8 left**, **8 right** (James Steveson), **15** (Conor Caffrey), **20**, **26** (Doug Martin); SuperStock/Kwame Zikomo p. **6**.

Cover photograph of an arrow road sign reproduced with permission of iStockphoto/Nicholas Belton; cover photographs of a lit cigarette in an ashtray and a single unlit cigarette reproduced with permission of Getty Images/PhotoDisc .

The publishers would like to thank Kostadinka Grossmith for her assistance in the preparation of this book.

Every effort has been made to contact copyright holders of any material reproduced in this book. Any omissions will be rectified in subsequent printings if notice is given to the publishers.

Disclaimer
All the Internet addresses (URLs) given in this book were valid at the time of going to press. However, due to the dynamic nature of the Internet, some addresses may have changed, or sites may have changed or ceased to exist since publication. While the author and publishers regret any inconvenience this may cause readers, no responsibility for any such changes can be accepted by either the author or the publishers. It is recommended that adults supervise children on the Internet.

Contents

Some words are shown in bold, **like this**. You can find out what they mean by looking in the Glossary.

What is tobacco?

Tobacco is a broad-leafed plant that is part of the nightshade family of plants. The tobacco plant contains a substance called **nicotine**. Nicotine is poisonous. A single drop of pure nicotine can kill a person in less than a minute. The small amounts of nicotine in tobacco products are not nearly enough to kill someone right away, but over time nicotine can do serious damage to a person's body.

Nicotine is also **addictive**. When people start using tobacco products, the nicotine will make them want to continue to use them. Tobacco users experience strong **cravings** and feel very uncomfortable if they try to stop using it. Tobacco has been shown to be as addictive as drugs such as **cocaine** and **heroin**.

NEWSFLASH

A study in 2003 found that addiction to nicotine may start the first time a person smokes. Thirteen-year-olds who had only smoked one or two cigarettes reported feeling cravings and other signs of addiction. This study supports the idea that it is very easy to become addicted to nicotine.

Tobacco is made from the dried and shredded leaves of the tobacco plant.

Tobacco comes in several different forms.

How is tobacco used?

Most people use tobacco by smoking the dried, shredded leaves in cigarettes. Dried tobacco can also be smoked in pipes and cigars. Some people smoke tobacco in flavoured cigarettes from India called *bidis*, or in Indonesian cigarettes flavoured with cloves, called *kreteks*.

Tobacco can also be chewed. People who chew tobacco do not swallow it. They chew it for a while and then spit it out. Chewing tobacco is made by forming leaves into blocks called plugs. Another kind of tobacco that is not smoked is called snuff. Snuff is made by grinding tobacco leaves into a fine powder. Snuff is held inside the mouth and then spat out. Some people inhale snuff into their nose.

The physical effects of smoking

When people smoke, they feel the effects of nicotine almost immediately. It takes less than ten seconds for nicotine to reach the brain. Nicotine causes the brain to produce chemicals that give the smoker a pleasant feeling. It can also make the smoker feel more alert or more relaxed.

Cigarette smoke goes directly into the lungs when it is inhaled. The smoke irritates the throat and the lungs. This can cause the smoker to cough and may make breathing more difficult, especially if the smoker has a cold or a breathing condition such as **asthma.**

Cigarette smoke irritates the throat and lungs.

Smoking and the body

Smoke is absorbed from the lungs into the bloodstream. The bloodstream carries nicotine to every organ in the body. Chewing tobacco is absorbed into the bloodstream through tissues in the mouth.

When a cigarette is burned, it produces a poisonous gas called **carbon monoxide.** Smokers inhale the carbon monoxide, which takes the place of some of the **oxygen** in the blood. All the organs and tissues in the body need oxygen to function properly. People who have a lot of carbon monoxide in their body from smoking may tire more easily than non-smokers when exercising. Heavy smokers may even experience vision problems or get headaches from carbon monoxide.

Smoking also causes **blood vessels** to **constrict** (get narrower), forcing the heart to work harder and **blood pressure** to rise. A smoker's heart rate may increase up to 30 percent while they are smoking.

Case Study

Kevin played on his school's football team. He was in top physical shape and could run 1.6 kilometres (one mile) in six minutes. Then he started smoking one pack of cigarettes a day. Soon he found it took eight minutes to run the same distance, and the running made him wheeze.

Trachea

Bronchus

Alveoli

Bronchiole

Cigarette smoke goes directly to the lungs, where it is absorbed into the bloodstream and carried to every organ in the body.

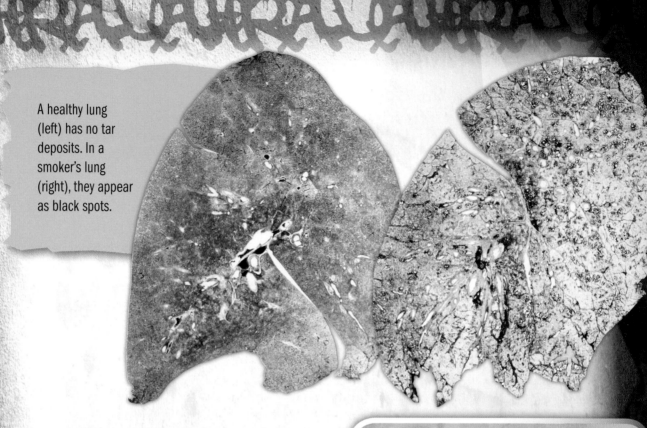

A healthy lung (left) has no tar deposits. In a smoker's lung (right), they appear as black spots.

Long-term effects

Tobacco smoke contains more than 4,800 chemicals, 69 of which are known to cause cancer. Some of these chemicals include:

- arsenic, an ingredient in rat poison
- ammonia, which is used in cleaning products
- turpentine, which is used for stripping paint
- butane, a component of gasoline
- formaldehyde, which is used to preserve dead bodies.

Cigarette smoke also contains tiny particles of **tar** that harden into a brown sticky substance in the lungs. Tar build-up in the lungs keeps them from functioning properly. It can lead to serious illnesses such as lung cancer and **emphysema**.

NEWSFLASH

Many smokers use cigarettes labelled "light" or "low tar" or smoke filtered cigarettes, believing that they are getting less nicotine and tar. Recent research has shown that these smokers are just as likely to get lung cancer and other smoking-related illnesses as other smokers. This may be because most smokers inhale more deeply when they smoke these cigarettes.

Smoker's cough

Inhaling smoke causes smokers to produce excess **phlegm**, which makes them cough. Many smokers develop a cough that never seems to go away completely, even when they are not smoking. Smokers also get sick more often than non-smokers – not just from diseases related to smoking, but also from other illnesses such as colds and flu. This is because smoking makes their **immune system** work less efficiently.

Smoking and appearance

Smoking changes the way a person looks. Tobacco can leave yellow stains on a person's teeth and fingernails. It can also damage gums and cause bad breath. In addition, smoking damages tiny blood vessels in the skin. Because the blood vessels are damaged, the skin does not get the oxygen and other nutrients it needs. This causes the smoker's skin to age faster.

Smokers cannot taste and smell things as well as non-smokers. Over time, smoking deadens a person's sense of taste and smell.

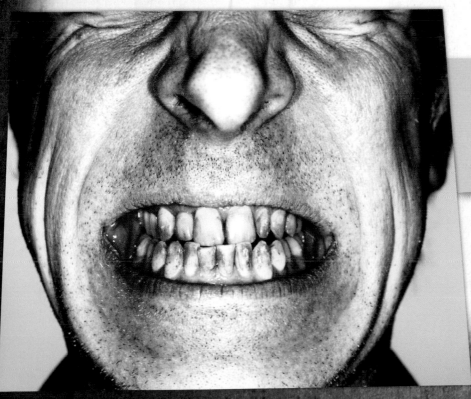

Tobacco stains teeth and damages gums.

Life-threatening illnesses

Smoking can do serious damage to the body. Smokers put themselves at risk of a variety of illnesses, and even death. Each year more than 110,000 people in the United Kingdom die prematurely from smoking-related illnesses. One in five deaths in the United Kingdom is related to smoking. That makes smoking the number-one cause of preventable deaths.

The chemicals in tobacco can cause cancer. The most common kind of cancer caused by smoking is lung cancer. Tobacco also causes cancers of the mouth, throat, stomach, kidney, **pancreas,** and **bladder,** as well as some kinds of **leukaemia.**

Smoking damages the tiny airways in the lungs and causes the lungs to become inflamed. Damaged and inflamed lungs can cause long-term and even permanent lung diseases, which include emphysema, **bronchitis,** and asthma.

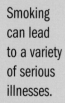

Smoking can lead to a variety of serious illnesses.

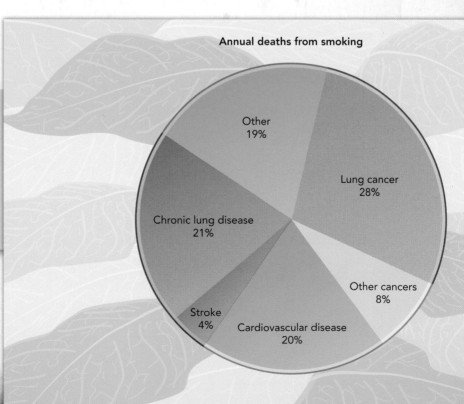

Annual deaths from smoking

Other
19%

Lung cancer
28%

Chronic lung disease
21%

Other cancers
8%

Stroke
4%

Cardiovascular disease
20%

The chemicals in tobacco products can also damage the heart and the blood vessels. These chemicals cause **plaque** to build up inside the blood vessels. Less blood can flow through blood vessels with plaque build-up, which can result in blood clots. Blood clots can lead to strokes and heart attacks. Smokers are twice as likely to die of a heart attack as non-smokers.

Smoking during pregnancy

Smoking can harm babies that are still in the womb. When a pregnant woman smokes, her smoking affects her unborn baby. Babies of mothers who smoke are more likely to be born dead than those of non-smokers. Babies of smoking mothers are also at risk of being born too small and of having poorly developed lungs.

Case Study

Gruen Von Behren started using chewing tobacco when he was 13 years old. At 17 he was diagnosed with cancer of the mouth. After many painful treatments and 40 surgeries, Gruen is still alive, but his face is severely disfigured. Gruen gives speeches at schools in America encouraging teens not to use tobacco products.

Tobacco products can cause disfiguring cancers, especially in the mouth and throat.

Social effects

Smoking affects the way a person lives his or her life. Most smokers find it difficult to go more than a few hours without a cigarette. Many smokers have their first cigarette within 15 minutes of waking up. A smoker who smokes a pack a day must find time to smoke 20 cigarettes throughout the day. Some smokers smoke two or even three packs every day.

Smoking bans

Finding a place to smoke has started to become more difficult. Many countries, such as Australia, the Republic of Ireland, and the United Kingdom, now have "smoke free" laws. In July 2007 a ban was put in place in England forbidding smoking in the workplace, at restaurants, and in other public places. Smoking is also banned on aeroplanes, trains, and buses, making long trips difficult for smokers.

In many places smoking is looked down on and smokers may be treated unfavourably. Many non-smokers do not want smokers to smoke in their home or car. Landlords may refuse to rent property to smokers.

People are no longer allowed to smoke in many public places.

Smoking bans force people who want to smoke at work to go outdoors to do it.

Teenage smokers

Teenagers who smoke may have more trouble in school than their non-smoking classmates. Smokers often get poor grades and are more likely to get suspended from school than non-smokers. In addition, teenagers who smoke are more likely to use drugs and alcohol than those who do not smoke.

Smoking is expensive. A pack of cigarettes costs about £5. That means that a pack-a-day smoker will spend about £150 each month on cigarettes – more than £1,800 each year!

Case Study

Emma started smoking when she was 14. She got her cigarettes from friends and then started buying them in a shop where they did not ask for identification. When the shop started checking identification, Emma waited outside the door and asked strangers to buy cigarettes for her.

Spending time in smoky places can be dangerous, even for non-smokers.

Second-hand smoke

Smoking does not just affect the smoker. A smoker inhales only a small amount of the smoke from a cigarette. The rest of the smoke pollutes the air. This smoke-polluted air is called second-hand smoke. People who are near a smoker end up breathing the second-hand smoke. By breathing in second-hand smoke, even non-smokers can experience some of the negative effects of smoking. We call this passive smoking.

Adult non-smokers who frequently breathe in second-hand smoke increase their risk of lung cancer and heart disease by 25 to 30 percent. Family members of smokers are often exposed to large amounts of second-hand smoke. Many non-smokers have become sick and even died because their spouses were smokers.

What do you think?

Many smokers believe they have the right to smoke wherever they want and that smoking bans limit their rights. Most non-smokers do not think they should have to breathe polluted air. Do you think smokers should be able to smoke wherever they want?

Second-hand smoke and children

Children are the greatest victims of second-hand smoke. In 1996, a study found that around 45 percent of children in the United Kingdom live in homes with at least one smoking adult. When parents or older siblings smoke around children, they are putting them at risk of asthma, ear infections, **pneumonia**, and bronchitis, as well as slowed lung growth. Smokers who live with non-smokers can help to keep their loved ones safe by smoking in another room or outdoors.

NEWSFLASH

The tobacco industry say more people will smoke at home when smoking is banned in public places. This would expose more children to second-hand smoke. This is not true in countries where bans are already in place.

Young children are often forced to breathe their parents' second-hand smoke.

15

Who uses tobacco?

The first people to use tobacco were the native people of North America and South America. In some tribes tobacco was only smoked in ceremonies and was used by leaders and healers. In other tribes tobacco use was more widespread. Christopher Columbus and other explorers brought tobacco back to Europe. Tobacco soon became a profitable crop for American colonists, who sold it in Europe and Asia. Today tobacco products can be found in almost every corner of the world.

At first no one knew that tobacco was harmful. Many people even thought it was healthy and could cure illnesses. More and more people began to smoke. During wartime, smoking increased even more. Soldiers received cigarettes along with food and other necessities in both World War I and World War II. Many young men entered the army as non-smokers and came out addicted to cigarettes.

In the 1950s most people did not know that smoking was dangerous.

Tobacco's peak

Smoking reached its peak in the 1960s, when the health risks to smoking became more well-known. In 1962 the **Royal College of Physicians** released a study showing that tobacco caused serious health problems. Most people were surprised to learn that smoking was dangerous. Many people quit immediately. In 1971 tobacco companies were required to put health warnings on products sold in the United Kingdom. These warnings state that using tobacco is dangerous. Since then, the percentage of smokers in the United Kingdom has decreased steadily.

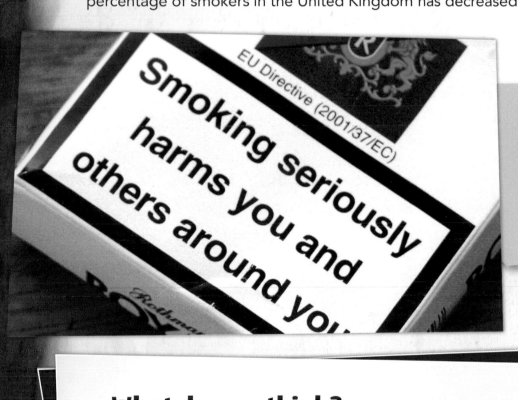

In 1971 tobacco companies were required to put warnings such as these on all their products.

What do you think?

For many years tobacco companies sold their products without telling the public about the dangers of smoking. Now people who have suffered serious illnesses or lost loved ones from smoking may **sue** tobacco companies. The tobacco companies say that people make their own choices and they have never forced anyone to smoke. Do you think tobacco companies should have to pay?

Who smokes today?

Around 10 million adults smoke in the United Kingdom. That is about one in every four people. Slightly more men smoke than women. People who have less money are also more likely to smoke. Poor people may be more likely to start smoking because they feel that even though smoking is expensive, it is one of the few pleasures they can afford. Once addicted, poor smokers may have a harder time quitting because they cannot afford therapies that are helpful for giving up cigarettes.

Education also plays a role. The more educated people are about the dangers of smoking, the less likely they are to smoke. In general, the less education a person has, the more likely they are to smoke.

Only adults aged 18 or older are allowed to buy tobacco products.

NEWSFLASH

A study completed in 2003 found that over half of underage smokers buy their cigarettes either by purchasing them themselves or by paying another person to buy them. Young smokers also get cigarettes from other people and about one in ten teenage smokers have stolen cigarettes from another person or from a shop.

One in five
15-year-olds
smokes tobacco
regularly.

Teenagers and children

Even though it is now illegal for people under 18 years old to buy or use tobacco products, many children still smoke. Over 80 percent of smokers start smoking as teenagers. In England, about one in five 15-year-olds is a regular smoker: 16 percent of boys and 25 percent of girls. In 2005, 9 percent of 11–15 year-olds reported that they were regular smokers.

Some young people prefer *bidis* and *kreteks* to cigarettes. They come in different flavours and children prefer their taste. Although many young people believe that bidis and kreteks are less dangerous than cigarettes, this is not true. *Bidis* and *kreteks* have higher levels of nicotine, tar, and carbon monoxide than cigarettes.

Why people smoke

No one plans to get addicted to cigarettes when they take their first puff, but that is exactly what happens to many young people. Every day around 450 children in the United Kingdom start smoking. Of these, more than 360 will become daily smokers. Around 80 percent of adult smokers started smoking as teenagers.

For many people smoking begins at home. Teenagers who live in homes where parents or siblings smoke are four times more likely to become smokers than those who live with non-smokers.

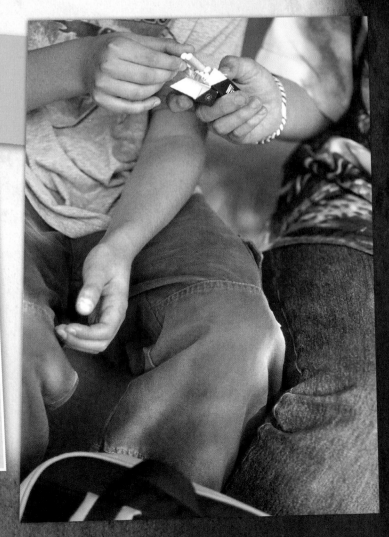

Teenagers often get cigarettes from their friends.

Case Study

Leah started smoking when she was just nine years old. She wanted to fit in with older kids who smoked. Most of Leah's family members are smokers and some of them have died from cancer. Leah is worried about her own smoking and wants to quit.

Many teenagers start smoking because they think it will help them make friends.

Peer pressure

Many teenagers start smoking because of **peer pressure.** Peer pressure is when one person makes another person feel that he or she must act or look a certain way in order to fit in. Teenagers often think that they will be rejected by a group or be made fun of if they do not smoke. Many teenagers find themselves addicted to cigarettes because they are afraid to say no.

Teenagers do not have to be afraid to say no. Most young people do not smoke. They will support their peers' decision not to smoke, too. Parents and teachers can also offer help and support for staying away from tobacco. Teenagers who are feeling the effects of peer pressure should find an adult that they like and trust to talk to. In addition teenagers should remember that there are much better ways to fit into a group than by smoking. Joining an after-school club or sports team is a fun and healthy way to make friends.

New laws mean that tobacco companies can no longer sponsor Formula One teams in European races.

Tobacco's targets

Tobacco companies know that most of their customers start smoking when they are young, so they create advertising that appeals to teenagers and children. In the late 1980s one tobacco company in the United States used a cartoon camel to promote its products. "Joe Camel" became as well known as Mickey Mouse, and cigarette sales skyrocketed.

Since 2003, most forms of tobacco advertising have been forbidden in the United Kingdom. It is now illegal for cigarette companies to advertise through TV, radio, the Internet, billboards, magazines, and newspapers. Advertising is also forbidden at sporting events, though it is allowed at some global events.

NEWSFLASH

In the past, one way that cigarette companies in the United States appealed to teenagers was by selling sweet- and fruit-flavoured cigarettes. But that will not happen anymore. In October 2006 tobacco companies were forced to take the flavoured cigarettes off the market.

Anti-smoking campaigns

Anti-smoking groups have fought back against the tobacco companies by launching several successful advertising campaigns. Their adverts encourage people not to smoke. Many groups are now using shock tactics to make the effects of smoking graphically clear. Recent campaigns have included cigarettes that drip fat to show how smoking can block the arteries; babies and young children breathing out smoke to show the effects of passive smoking; and people with hooks in their mouths to show how addictive smoking is.

Anti-smoking advertising has become so powerful that it is now one of the most effective ways of persuading people to stop smoking. In 2004 a study showed that 32 percent of attempts to quit smoking were prompted by anti-smoking adverts, while doctors prompted just 21 percent of attempts.

Anti-smoking adverts are an effective way to teach people about the dangers of smoking.

No more nicotine

Most smokers know that tobacco is bad for them and want to quit. Seventy percent of teenage smokers say they wish that they had never started smoking. However, nicotine is extremely addictive and quitting is difficult. Every year 40 percent of smokers try to quit, but only five percent succeed on their first try. These numbers look discouraging, but even smokers who fail should not give up. Most smokers try and fail several times before finally stopping for good.

Quitting is difficult because the cravings for a cigarette and **withdrawal** symptoms are usually very intense. Withdrawal symptoms occur because a smoker's body is physically dependent on nicotine. When the body is deprived of nicotine, a smoker can experience a wide variety of symptoms, including:

- depression
- irritability
- trouble sleeping
- trouble concentrating
- restlessness
- headache
- upset stomach
- tiredness
- increased appetite.

Quitting smoking is difficult, but it can be done.

The most severe withdrawal symptoms usually disappear within a few days. The rest of the symptoms and cravings fade over a period of weeks, although smokers can experience cravings years after they smoked their last cigarette.

People who quit smoking feel healthier and can perform better athletically.

Top Tips

The March of Dimes gives these tips to teenagers who want to quit smoking:

- Write down why you want to stop smoking.
- Choose a "Quit Day" some time in the next two weeks.
- Ask a non-smoking friend or sibling to help you quit.
- Throw out all cigarettes, ashtrays, matches, and lighters on your "Quit Day."
- Stay away from places and activities that make you want to smoke.

Case Study

After three years of smoking, Dan quit when he was 19. He wanted to quit while he was still young so that his lungs would not be permanently damaged. Five months after quitting he is thrilled that he can swim and play tennis better because his lungs are healthier.

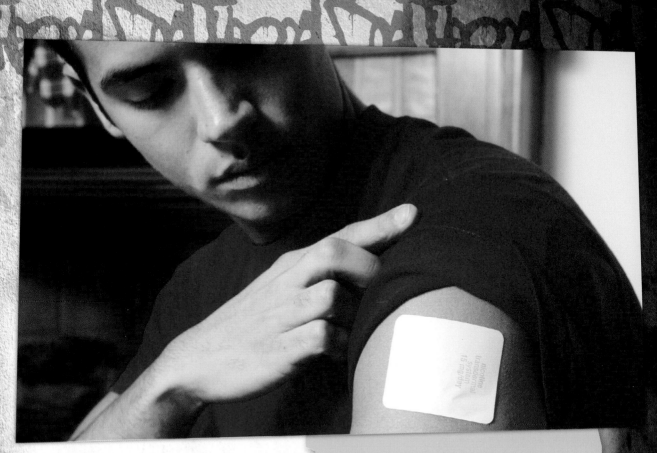

Nicotine replacement therapies like patches can help people to stop smoking.

Ways to quit

There are many ways to stop smoking, and different methods work for different people. Smokers often try to go "cold turkey". This means giving up all forms of nicotine at once. It results in severe withdrawal symptoms, which start within a few hours of smoking the last cigarette. Withdrawal symptoms make going cold turkey difficult, but if a smoker can make it through the first 72 hours, the worst of the symptoms disappear. Going cold turkey is the quickest way to get nicotine out of the body.

Top Tips

If your parents smoke at home, they are putting your health at risk as well as their own. Even if they want to quit, they may need encouragement to take the first step. Why not try asking them to quit? Make sure you explain why you would like them to quit, and try not to get angry. Let them know that their health is important to you. Quitting smoking is difficult, even for adults, so offer to help and support them as they try to quit.

Nicotine replacement therapy

Using nicotine replacement therapy is another way to quit smoking. Instead of smoking, the person uses a nicotine replacement such as a nicotine patch, nasal spray, or chewing gum. These give the user a limited amount of nicotine. Over a period of weeks or months, the amount is gradually reduced until the user is no longer addicted to nicotine.

Some people find that using the non-nicotine drugs **bupropion** and **varenicline** can reduce withdrawal symptoms. These drugs must be prescribed by a doctor and can be used along with other methods.

Most people who quit say that support from family and friends is important. Many people also benefit from individual or group counselling. Free telephone "hotlines" that people can call for advice and support are available 24 hours a day.

Tobacco hotlines offer support for people who are trying to quit smoking.

Saying no to tobacco

Even though you know that using tobacco products is dangerous and addictive, it may still be hard to say no when a friend offers you a cigarette. Here are some tips for dealing with peer pressure.

First, remember:

- You do not have to do anything that you do not want to do.

- It is perfectly okay to say no. You do not owe anyone an explanation.

- Most young people do not smoke, so you are in good company.

- It is a good idea to have an answer ready for someone who offers you a cigarette. Try to find a reason to say no that is true for you.

- If you are allergic to smoke or if you do not like the smell, you can use that as a reason for not smoking.

- If you will get in trouble from your parents for smoking, you can give that as a reason.

- If your parents or someone you know smokes, you can talk about how you would like them to quit, so you do not smoke yourself.

- You can always say that smoking can kill you and cause serious diseases such as cancer.

Real friends will respect your decision, but if someone will not stop pressuring you to smoke, it is okay to ask for help from an adult you trust, such as a teacher or parent.

Tobacco facts

- Around 10 million adults smoke in the United Kingdom. That is just over 25 percent of the population, or one in every four people.

- Eighty percent of adult smokers started smoking as teenagers.

- Every day nearly 450 children try smoking for the first time. Of these, 360 become daily smokers.

- Twenty percent of 15-year-olds in the United Kingdom are regular smokers. Nine percent of 11–15 year-olds are regular smokers.

- Among Australian adults, 19 percent of men and 16 percent of women are daily smokers. However, more 17-year-olds are smokers – about 24 percent.

- Each year more than 110,000 people in the United Kingdom die prematurely from using tobacco products.

- One in every five deaths in the United Kingdom is smoking-related.

- Half of all teenagers who are currently smoking will die from diseases caused by tobacco if they continue to smoke.

- Nearly 45 percent of children in the United Kingdom live in homes with at least one smoking adult.

- Adult non-smokers who frequently breathe second-hand smoke increase their risk of lung cancer and cardiac disease by 25 to 30 percent.

- About 12,000 people in the United Kingdom die from passive smoking each year.

- Smokers are more likely to use drugs and alcohol than non-smokers.

- A smoker who smokes a pack of cigarettes a day spends more than £1,800 each year on cigarettes. Many smokers smoke more than a pack a day.

Glossary

addictive something that causes the body to become dependent on it

asthma usually chronic lung condition which causes coughing, wheezing, and breathing problems

bladder bag-like organ where urine is stored before it leaves the body

blood pressure pressure of the blood against the walls of the blood vessels

blood vessel tube in the body which carries blood to tissues and organs

bronchitis disease caused by the swelling of the bronchial tubes in the lungs

bupropion prescription drug used to treat depression or help a person quit smoking tobacco

carbon monoxide poisonous gas

cocaine illegal and highly addictive drug derived from the coca plant

constrict to make narrower

craving an extremely strong desire

emphysema serious disease in which the air sacs in the lungs become enlarged and damaged, making breathing difficult

heroin illegal and highly addictive drug derived from the pain reliever morphine

immune system the body's system for protecting itself from illness and disease

leukaemia often fatal form of cancer in which the body produces too many white blood cells

nicotine poisonous and addictive substance found in the tobacco plant

oxygen gas that is essential for life

pancreas large gland behind the stomach that helps the body digest food

peer pressure social pressure to behave or look a certain way in order to be accepted by a group

phlegm thick mucus secreted by the respiratory system

plaque deposits of fatty material that build up on the inner walls of blood vessels

pneumonia illness in which the lungs become inflamed

Royal College of Physicians the oldest medical society in England. It aims to improve standards of medical practice and give advice on medical and health matters.

sue take legal action against someone

tar dark, sticky residue from tobacco smoke

varenicline prescription drug that can reduce the withdrawal symptoms when a person stops smoking tobacco

withdrawal unpleasant physical and emotional symptoms that occur when a person gives up a substance on which he or she was dependent

Further resources

Books

The Biography of Tobacco, Carrie Gleason (Crabtree Publishing Company, 2006)

Harmful Substances (Keeping healthy), Carol Ballard (Hodder Wayland, 2007)

Smoking (It's your health), Judith Anderson (Watts, 2004)

Websites

ASH
http://www.ash.org.uk

Go smoke free
http://www.gosmokefree.co.uk

Kids Against Tobacco Smoke
http://www.roycastle.org/kats

Quit Victoria
http://www.quit.org.au

Organizations

NHS Smoking Helpline
Tel: 0800 169 0 169

British Lung Foundation
73-75 Goswell Road
London EC1V 7ER
Website: www.lunguk.org

Action on Smoking and Health Australia
PO Box 572
Kings Cross
NSW 1340
Australia
Website: www.ashaust.org.au

Index